# THIS IF ANYTHING

## POEMS PAINTINGS

PHILIP HUTTON

# Publication Data

First Published 2009

ISBN 978-0-9562884-0-0

Published by
P B Hutton, 84 High Street, Peebles, Scottish Borders EH45 8SW

Printed by
Kelso Graphics, The Knowes, Kelso, Scottish Borders TD5 7BH

Philip Hutton was born in Peebles in 1949. He studied Drawing and Painting at Gray's School of Art, Aberdeen, and has painted and exhibited in England and Scotland. He taught art in Scottish Borders primary schools for many years, then freelanced as an art tutor and lecturer in history of art. He has written poems since 2002.

# Contents

# Arran

The island smoulders in its lingering light
and nothing  breaks the lapping of the waves
but the silver brimming of the tidal night

a harbour shivers in remembered light
peaks vibrate, the fallen rocks and caves
gash the faultline steep with bracken blight

fifty years ago we left the island, right
perhaps to taste a wider world and wave
away those sea-limits to our sight

but island images still float, despite
propitiating watercolours, something craves
repayment of the primal debt, to slight

the breach of time, and take delight
in chasmal breath, in breast-high wave
to vindicate the bourne of unlensed sight.

The island smoulders in its cleansing light
And nothing breaks the slapping of the waves
But my white arms which sweep and fight
To find the swimming of the tidal night.

# Holiday Snap

A serious bike, blackened with precautions,
armoured oilbath chaincase, mudguards and chromeplate,
and cable brakes clutched in a blur of motion
snapped by a tumbled dyke and a farm gate.

This cycle so confidently handed on
from father to son via elder brother
in thrift and stewardship for all time to come;
such all-steel assumptions, the reality quite other.

What thorough checking, fittings, lighting, braking
not for this summer only (just doing as he likes!)
but all proper businesses and undertakings
that come at last to boys on bikes.

Bareheaded, barekneed, down a dirt lane in Galloway
breezily flogging his father's sombre Raleigh.

# How I found three quarters of an inch

Boys just outgrown their teddy bears
but not yet cuddling Renoirs or Ferraris
practise choosing:
I want the red one
Thirteen's my lucky number
       -   what's yours? Hearts or Hibs?

Bothered by all this choice
I scanned the mascot heraldry of love objects
       -   nothing doing.
But the ruler fiddled
my fingers and sightlines
with its own worn calibrations.

What was it about three quarters of an inch
that needed my adoption?
Totty Tom Thumb limits
tight-pinched ¾ in
broadened into five words,
precise, arbitrary and disembodied.
The class moved on to Africa.

# Chums for Life

Our mother's and father's social energy
drew their friends to dinner, and then we
allowed to listen, pass the salt, and be
like smaller icebergs on a polar sea.

Those bluffs rode their own deep swell
of chance, affinity or happenstance as well
as loyalty to some past school or university,
the golf, the staffroom, the War, the Thirties
the barnacled recital, launched and leading
usually to politics, and getting rid of Eden.

I thought of school, bible stories about gardens
and their strange restrictions and expulsions,
of sometime chums gone to the enemy
and boys unaskable, somehow, home for tea.

But grown-up friendship, that formal dance
of decades farragoed with their provenance
seemed diffuse, colossal, ocean dispositions
and we children only recent acquisitions
newly fitted up and plumbed into the works,
expected morning-bright to earn our marks.

# The Face

I knew at six my face a fudge
a flaccid formless pink confection
all lips, curls, mottled cheeks
wobbling up to the mirror's edge.
Horrid curls! Undisattributably mine as breeks
Tugged and fingered at front door inspection.

Considering that face of mine,
its original stupidity now modified at fifty-eight,
articulated, grammatically rendered, better phrased
by wrinkles, bags and bulges, worry lines,
the thoughtful specs, the greying hair now praised,
waved like a tide, the prodigal, the tax rebate.

# Match

I fling lit matches at gasfilled bubbles.
The cooker (only used in summer) has
an igniting nozzle to dip in soap,
they swell and lift.
Perhaps I am a little old for childish games,
Twelve, old enough to remember zeppelins.
Spent matches must be removed
and the sulphur cleared from the skies.

Now Walter Pater tells me I should burn
with a hard gemlike flame,
more like a gasring than those haphazard flares;
smouldering like a late-victorian James Dean,
hiding the scorn behind a heavy moustache.
I am nineteen and do not feel the need
of the moustache.

That can wait until I'm thirty-five
And smoking heavily.

# Flash Flood

She was the last to cross that bridge
they said, froze as the tarmac cracked
the wee dog skedaddling from the edge
to leatherhaul her to the safer ledge.
The froth rose high as the arch unpacked.

Time passed, a strong new concrete span
and the old lady, with dog, that festive day
was first to cross, according to the plan –
with councillors, a ribbon, photographers, a band,
and all the works and wonders of celebrity.

Was I the last to cross my bridge?
Cracks appeared in the curriculum.
Categories, undermined an age
disintegrated in a flash of rage.
My tottering passage seemed ridiculous.

Think again these metaphors. What flood?
What bridge? Only a middle-aged assumption
that whatever mess one made, instead
the working out would be for good,
an arch held up by wit and glue and gumption.

But earlier there were furies calling
dream invoking, fact despising
for a crashed pose, held, but stalling.
Always the ground beneath me falling
And the low froth boiling, rising.

# Flitting

Flitting and fitting to a new dimension
means fleeing flats and flat-life under roofs
to fetch up flat upright behind outfacing wall,
finding new ways in fluedark stairs, standing proofs
of firebight rooms, stacked in vertical extension
for old furniture's new niche to uncoil and fall.

Flats framed my days as thirty years went by
longer recall, deep as Children's Hour or the Last Tram
brings back tall terrace houses, crammed with neighbours;
longest, the springloaded reflex of the swaying pram.
Now treetop-high on stilts of time I try
still, to shape new space for future labours.

Facing the stonebuilt street, but hiding down the back
a crumbling yard, and crooked steps which give
déjà vu, to fruit trees, as painted in the sixties
of the nineteenth century, blue garden gate, little river
that parallels the street. Up this perpendicular track
I scan all my houses, all change, all fixity.

# Shrinking Caravaggio

Caravaggio! Master of white sweat
and stunned illumination large as life.
These swagger martyrs twist and fret,
commit their saintly guts to holy strife.

A drooping canvas hung behind a rail
was what I found in France, and here it seems
much further shrunk to art-book scale
under a table lamp, and the surface gleam.

Shrunk? Surely, and good riddance to that whopping
whining kniving god-bothering feverous stare.
I study details in an armchair after shopping,
answering the telephone and smoothing down my hair.

What is to be done with Caravaggio's sweat?
It puts a shine on the antithesis, our recent
intellectual mentors, polished calm and neat,
secular, long-lived, respectable and decent.

# The Coldstream Climate

As Principal, Slade School of Art
or on the Board of Governors of the BBC
or that of the National Gallery
or the Whitechapel Gallery
or of the Opera at Covent Garden
or on the Committee for Government Purchase
or that of Protective Custody
in Event of War, of Works of Art
or on the London Parochial Charities Board;
in the Chair of the National Advisory Council for Art Education
or the National Council for Diplomas in Art and Design
or on the paint-streaked one
by the easel

he exacted
calibrations
stretched out an arm
to mark with an X
a point where light
or official attitude
shifts.

Consider this dead painter
shrouded in public offices
whose portraits once scaffolded
the suits heads and hands
of provosts and commissioners
in subsecting stations
intersecting spheres

never to be explained, flattered or interpreted
never to break the surface of the canvas.

His private necessity, elusive yet compelling
To weave the vivid stitches of perception
Into a sustaining fabric, credible and enduring.

*Note:*   *Phrases in the last section of the poem are borrowed from an*
    *essay on Sir William Coldstream by Sir Lawrence Gowing.*

# In Tate Modern

Open skies close on me
spirits freeze in me
corridors channel me
trenchlike around the re-
barbative hulks of art.

Only cafeterial measures
and window seat pleasures
the view to St Paul's, we
soak to our souls the re-
actionary sulks of art.

Wren's dome, Whistler's river
Trained my gaze, and if ever
again I gaze shall I see
new Being or just this re-
calcitrant bulk of art?

# Art Class

Expressiveness is not waiting there to be learned
any more than intelligence or creativity.
We do not reify. Something to be earned
is accuracy perhaps, observation, material skills.
What you might express is still peculiar to you,
not some view on art, however subtle or shrill,
but your buried river, your fleet proclivity
beneath the chartered streets, flashing fast and true,
this energy, like water gurgling back, a burn
back in original green, bursting from the hills.

You think you have (and here you may be wrong)
the aboriginal passion, the private soul so strong
that paint alone will find out what of this remains.
Watch no more television, especially not the news.
Work instead, this way, that way, push and strain,
read classic criticism and ephemeral reviews,
visit the Prado, the great galleries and the small,
have opinions, tell them, minds change after all,
lose your temper, but keep the sketchbooks full,
fill a shelf with them, and to the easel, tall
over the upright canvas, turn your face again.

You think you have (and this might be mistaken)
no particular originality or talent in the making;
but painting's like a voltage whose direction can be switched
for those who bring attention only find themselves enriched.
So you're free of bruising ego, poised and undistracted.
You make your own hogbristle touch
come clear and clear with practice.

# Song

Let the soppy-eyed soprano wallow
   in the Bluthner's shiny bay,
let the stub-armed 'companist come follow
   wild melismas sing and play.

Let the stooped piano blacksmith
   stumpenfingered strike F minor
while the lovelorn lady luckless
   leaps high C to scorn a whiner.

Bold cold hero! Warm weak lover!
   Let them swap their thin disguises.
Seething pianist lashes Bluthner
   knows the score, makes his surmises.

# In a Canadian Art Gallery

Beyond foyers and fountains
I walk the installations
from  room to room to room
and come to the booming dark
and the bright-lit space.
Another text on another wall,
foot-high letters floor to ceiling
and on around the corner
setting out the blogsite maunderings
of some expletive-intensified obsessive
with the not unexpected
toilet rolls set out on tables
to Make a Statement.
I shrug through a glass door

       Here

forty loudspeakers on forty stands
man-high face inwards
a forty foot cable-clustered ring.
Each propped black box, I gather,
wired to one recorded voice.
Come close! Listen in!
It breathes, sniffs, hums a bit
And clears an unseen throat,
sounding English. I see a sky
and all the pom-poms, rustlings swell
into a forest of invisibles.

       Now

out of this dark, one sings to me,
a voice high on one slow word
held to a note on a slender stand,
and one and another break out
as signals puse down all their cables,
and chasing the voices I carry my hearing
across a dozen segments of the ring
until the seven choirs gather up
sopranos mezzos altos, tenors one and two,
they float augustly to the upper sphere
breathing such balloons of harmony,
proclaiming new heights full and by,
the surge-bass of groundswell.
Thomas Tallis   -   Spem in Alium
Motet installed in forty parts.

*Note:      The Motet installation is by Janet Cardiff*

# Mme Landowska

Wanda Landowska plays the harpsichord
shuffles her pack of stainless steel
chords modulate round the harmonic wheel
like diamond trumps in every deal
all equal tempered to the sharpest card.

As Mme Landowska on the harpsichord
parades crack regiments formed in squares,
the helmets, straps, the cloak each Cossack wears,
gravel crunching boots, epaulettes plumes and flares
flash on the eye, the arquebus and sword.

Mme Landowska's school of harpsichord,
Paris, nineteen forty, fraught with fear,
she remained with one recording engineer
to save what might be saved of her career
and spend on disc what time she could afford.

When Mme Landowska plays the harpsichord
the engraving stylus on the spinning wax
records the thump, the drumming click and clack,
Scarlatti's trills on keyboards white and black
the shakes and creaks behind each spreading chord.

Wanda Landowska's sweetest una corda
was shadowed eastward by a German shell,
the stylus entered that dark stain as well,
a window rattled down, some chimneys fell.
She held on to the turning of a mordant.

When jew Landowska played her harpsichord
with fascist armies forty miles away
she recorded one more piece, but did not stay,
flipped shut her suitcase – labelled USA –
made Boulogne, found ship, and slipped aboard.

Mme Landowska plays the harpsichord.
I hear her now on walkman up by Lyne.
She lets her measure broaden into four-four time
and as she hits her stride I lengthen mine
full sixty years beyond the scars of war.

Now when Landowska plays the harpsichord
sonatas of Scarlatti, round it comes again
the intrusive crump, the sounding stain,
unshaken yet, the music's high disdain –
her slender instrument, and mightier than the sword.

# Lunchtime Concert

I lean the bike and clip the lock.

The music of Sebastian Bach intact
after the long dismantling of his faith
returns intentness to his writing act
fuelled by broth prepared with chicken stock,
oxygenated by an eighteenth century breath.

I release the bike and let the mind unblock.

# Skye

and
left and right
orotund and booming
cliffs and towers
shout and bang
at me and my shadow
shake and rattle
my boots and wits
that scale and scope
such mirroring and mountain

silent and black
they fill and form
the frame and the picture
from the peep o f the sky

# Skye

and
right and left
booming and orotund
towers and cliffs
bang and shout
at my shadow and me
rattle and shake
my wits and my boots
that scope and scale
such mountain and mirroring

black and silent
they form and fill
the picture and the frame
to the peep o f the sky

# Into Quiraing

So all day long we headed for Quiraing
with no clear picture of these 'sundered lava spills'
just the strange name linked with basalt walls
and bulging crags that jut and overhang.
A walker's path that slanted into rock terrain
and fright of cliff-edge drop, saw-toothed thrills
of vertigo, and skylined we four walked until
down chasmal plunge we saw that soft green plain.
Later, homeward turned, we still aspired to see
engulfed from underneath those feral spires,
hauling our bodies up the sliding scree
to what? Ossianic shades, chthonic pyres?
Eagles circled sure enough, but we felt light and free,
Swathed utterly, and soothed by stereolithic fires.

# The Warden

It is a Mole-endy house
silent, trim and waiting
lacking habitation only
though cushioned to the hilt,
pictured, glazed and charmed.

Attentive, I dribble water from a jug
moving around the potted plants
that breathe across the room,
read the meter, collect the letters
and clunk the door behind me.

Someone deposited a generation here
a phased lifetime grown viscous,
hung chime bars to test the still air
and left, caught a plane.

I shift within me
deeper, more opaquely sunk
such dark mezzanines,
lock-ups from long ago
superceded, blocked off and yet
with a warden on retainer.
Disclosed, in the strewn
charactery of dreams:
gifts of dust
crumbled papers
a shrouded overcoat
stiff as a board.

*Mole End:        Kenneth Graham, Wind in the Willows chapter 5*

# Collecting

A face turns a switch
somewhere in the foldaways of memory
where legions more, synapse-bound, subsist
as nameless as before, neither neighbour
nor close kin to me, but half-familiar townsfolk
who kept their alibis under their coats,
served in certain shops, frequented certain walks
and will not be met with now
in supermarket or car park.

Lanes of slight recollection teem
with signal traffic seeking destinations.

I think of wavelengths, magnetic oscillations
which, now filled to saturation
by our mobiles, routers, radios,
once hung empty in the skies
anticipating Marconi, Hertz and Reith.

Could our burden of defunct and lapse
posit in such interstices
across the wold of time
some active residue, beaming out perhaps
like nuclear waste, half-life lapping sheer away
into ampler foldings of the everyday?

# Anniversary (for Robina)

A rack of books, a shelf of tales
tatty covers, shockers, letters,
essays stuffed with cuttings
print leaking from the edges
crushed maps and hidden stuff behind.

You tug, you try to ease one out –
the gap clams up at once
Fontana Press, Penguins squashed
from the left end, pushing up to

All Change! Ten volumes stretch to Now

Tomes slide calm from their snug slots
fist wide, arm deep into the dark.
Thumping covers chill your palm –
set one down on cool mahoganny -
the bulk splits whitely outward
pages slide in reams, flop open to behold

     a cornucopia:
     travels inventories voices
     rooms coalsmoke
     recycling bags, bikes
     and all the rest

An image and a reckoning
of our ten years of marriage
and the time before for both and each,
a midlife edition – broad margined
bound and bound over into something
unsettled as to whether fiction fable or discourse.

We'll pack it up like a spent picnic
hampered and shouldered high, to be
slotted back on the open shelf.

Volume Eleven
on the next shelf
behind the glass door
which time will unlock?

# Evening Song

| | | |
|---|---|---|
| westering | river | lapping    into the  arches |
| homely | town | buttoned  into   its   hills |
| outlying | houses | seeping into    the  green |
| serried | roofs | cuddling  into    parallels |
| crusty | bread | buttered  into the  grain |
| insect | tractor | stitching  into patchwork |
| needle | steeple | gulls stepping  into    air |
| windy | avenue | browning  ino  embroidery |

Wanderer of fixed address
hurries by as time grows less
paths strewn where wind rotates
leaves spin, float, agitate,
scans album leaves as thick as plates
for what the archive illuminates
and long play records play as long
as will resuscitate the scent and song
that mourns the lost and primal state.
Beechen branches droop, may rest
but not the wanderer of fixed address.

the Moral Community?
        too grand by half  -  a drummed-up phrase
                but see the sunset on the water blaze!

These are the evening lands, that go under when the sun drops.

our circle gathers in the house by the river
not, these days, with the long-playing gramophone records
the symphonies, the concerti of our great years
but with the children, we talk about the children
and how our tables expanded for the grandchildren
                                as if we had secured their future
                                and their lives gave us joy

# Three Pains in Order of Severity

A dog turned nasty once and bit me on the lip.
O feel the quick squeezed sharpness of the canine rip
and see (God!) scattered drops and hear them drip.
But hands, towels take now and smother the quaking person,
swooning sympathy floods in, and strangers' excitation.
Regret the mess, of course, but spot the brute elation.

Extraction of a wisdom tooth, the aching lower right
impresses through dulled nerves the dentist's wristy might
squeezed hot through pliers, so chunky and so bright.

But cramp, cramp, cramp the calf squeezed inside out
a howdumbdeid of sinews wrenched about!
This nightmare muscling into consummation  -
This canonbusting opera of incarceration      -
This chained Fidelio's visitation.

# Do I remember Wick?

You whose forebear left there long ago
and never having been there yourself
would like the fishy rusty smell
to mellow your own folk memory......

Well, that time in Lyth when
the four of us set out for Wick,
my friends and I all very thick
together with her from Philadelphia.....

Well yes, those High Street shops,
the little park, the Sinclair monument
the harbour's mouldering accoutrements
a dinky tearoom to spread ourselves

about, and have a round of tea and cake
good talk, shop talk, gossip, mirth
about transatlantic muddles and so forth
cross-cultural civilities of give and take.....

You ask what I recall of Wick.........
I hesitate, trying to make light
of that which blocked the place from sight
that trick, that oddity of recall, fantastic....

A mere freakishness, a so-what, and yet to
use a trendy idiom the elephant
in the room, this girl from Philadelphia,
whose charm, friendliness, fine features

fine brain too, nothing would avail......
no, nothing shameful or embarrassing,
we joked about it, not harassing
her, but coy about our own small scale......

but I, most of all, sensed the burden
of it, the unavoidable and present fact
though she just waved it by, dignity intact,
a less than trivial misfortune........

It's just that she was six feet nine........
This photo........we stand in an uneven line.

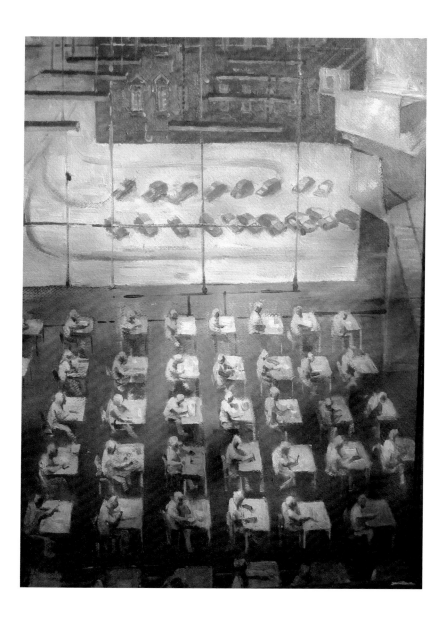

# Five Compete for the Moral High Ground

Good English? What, for these poor creatures?
See it from their side! That one cowers
daily traumatised by jeering, clouting,
fear of knives, the stepfather's hammer.
Why should he be made to stumble
into pettifogging pits of grammar?
Apostrophes! About as meaningless as shouting
in a foreign tongue.  Abuse their powers,
repressive presbyterian pedant teachers!

   Yes, I comprehend the blighted features
   and pity even the blank-eyed stepfather,
   traumatised in his turn, time out of mind,
   ricket-legged dwarf-tongued from the slum,
   why should he apologise and mumble
   liberal decencies never done to him?
   His deep grudge must smoulder blind
   firing up the itch to smash rather
   than mealy-mouth the spiel of teachers.

      I pity all our fellow creatures,
      the fleeing dispossessed of Africa
      scorched by the not unexpected rage
      of rampant soldiery, legacy of empires.
      Trailing past our cameras they stumble
      over frontiers held by genocidal vampires,
      stateliness ruled so casually in the age
      of our Victorian forebears, traffickers
      in ivory, colonial rule, bible preachers.

Ah, my feelings somewhat exceed yours,
I did the Auschwitz tour, so torn
I was for the poor Jews, the Jews stripped
to the gold fillings, I quiver at their fate
imagining the clanking cattle-trucks rumble
to the camps, past the wire-crowned gate.

  My heart bleeds for Jesus, scourged and whipped
  The most kingly victim, trumped with thorns.
  I feel it all, my feelings are my teachers.

# Dialectic

When you and I hit politics
two congeries face and blink
reveries  fantasies  histories
the mobs of the most secret cities
slitting dictionaries
to find the hardest word for it.

When we hear each other spout
(Bush, Hurraishi, Iran Iraq)
I, reciprocating, tough it out;
you getting good at getting back
to crowbar up my argument.

If wrong, as indeed I think you are,
the blame will not go very far,
the shades and clients of the just
will note incontinent phenomena,
millions erupt because they must.

But I, if my sums go askew,
my stuff goes right on the cart
past paupers' graves and smothering ash
past the scapegoat and the Dead Sea stew
to the landfill
with recycling bins for semi-trash.

# The New Cars

We propose that the government issues
new cars for all who choose to have them.
Free cars, cheap fuel, convenient parking,
waivers of the coming congestion charges,
priority at traffic lights and preference
at all bottlenecks, checkpoints, spotchecks,
filters, barriers in or out
of drive-in beauy spots.

We'll have the new cars built in Coventry
a million in the first batch,
rolling solid-tyred from the factory,
heavy bodied in unbending steel
and painted only grey or grey.
Squat as pugs or as Ford Pops and
slow, only forty-five perhaps.
But clean, collectivised
and hydrogen powered.

The aim is to offend, and be reviled
by motorists conditioned to the old ways.
Market forces, manifold choice, self-expression
in metal, the old geezers can go their way
dressed in go-faster stripes
take their chances and their libidos
in the old botched utopia.

# Prospect

A bright new bike, so light and lean and keen
with one-inch tyres that skite through shining rain,
dropped handlebars, the rider humped and thin
encompassing the city and the plain.

With modest legpower derailleured into fugues –
top gear augments the speed at half the beat and still
exacts a space to inch past blocks and traffic queues –
the needle-like assertion of the choosing will.

As Milton's Satan put on swift wings and soared
to Chaos' towering concave high, so likewise
this halogen rider plumbs the night, to steer
his lanelight underneath the inky skies.

Confidently rational, now inspired by prophesy –
Anticipate hegemony!  His proper name is Lucifer.

# Windows

I walked out on a fine spring morning
met no-one, loitering nor hurried, nor were the hills
alive with the Sound of Music, nor spake a Voice
from a Burning Bush, nor perched the Byronic type
over a Sea of Fog from convenient rocky top.
       Free from all that clutter
under the empty godless clarity of sky
the minimal furnishing of the green valley
and cool silence for the thought-voices,
the living and the dead, presence sparked
in ratruns through the head

and from a recalled twist of track
a gravelled accent blown toward me-
resonant reiterated phrase, molecularly marked
words heard on Walkman once, years back.

Sheepruns slanted to a minor summit,
I'd tea from a flask and chocolate
and I raised my eyes to a vapour trail
       dragged across the blue
the craft seemed close at thirty thousand feet
its steely underside reflecting sunlit land,
beyond, so chill and void, the sky.

Turned about I glimpsed the steepled town
far off, neat as a tapestry, hill-foot spread.
Hill-solitude I carried down the road
past the thirty sign, the villas, bungalows
       a stranger muttered by
the park, the river footbridge, up gated steps
to where of course the singing found me
       sidelong by the church
throated from high windows, dark and packed
like swelling heat, an oven left on overnight,
the faithful, presumably upstanding in their pews
praising the not-forgotten in the highest
and on the High Street, bootsteps echoed back.

# On Hearing the Results of the
# Radio 4 Poll of Favourite Paintings

1805    For England expects every man to do his duty

1838    And Turner, smitten with it, sketching
          that sunset from the Margate ferry

1843    And Ruskin dips his pen and pauses over beauty

1905    And Hutton, Philip B, engineer, ancestor of mine,
          and amateur painter, there in Trafalgar Square

1939    And Sir Kenneth Clark, troubled before the Fighting Temeraire

2005    Now click the website to the poll on Radio Four

1939    Knowing those empty mines in Wales will harbour in the dark

1905    Carrying Haeckel's best-seller
          The Riddle of the Universe at the Close of the Nineteenth Century

1843    "Under the blazing veil of vaulted fire
          which lights the vessel on her last path….."

1838    At the gunwhale also Woodington, sculptor of the column's base

1805    Nelson's column Victory, Temeraire, the rest in line astern

1838    A pair of tugs, not one, was needed in this case

1843    "there is a blue, deep, desolate hollow of darkness….."

1905    Flyleaf open for colour notes:
          lead-grey, carmine, umber furthest, orange near

1939    Old masters, today in their places only until closing time

2005    Or is there still a listening community
          with all of Turner between their ears?

1939    A column of battleship-grey vans out there
          Shadowing the gallery as far as Admiralty Arch

1905   And the book sails out with him next day to Petersburg

1843   "out of which you can hear the voice of the night wind…."

1838   Sheerness to Deptford, a breaker commissioned at grimy Rotherhithe

1805   Let us be masters of the Channel for six hours says Bonaparte, and
        we are Masters of the world

1838   With gamboges, fiery carmine, cadmium and cochineal

1843   "And the dull boom of the disturbed sea;
        because the cold shadows are gathering through every sunbeam…."

1905   Those notes
        and a monochrome stampsize picture to work from

1939   And queer enough to the eyes of the last loiterers on the steps

2005   Now the great canvas spread of estuary pulls in a tide
        Of love and electronic votes, the loyal Constable second in line

1939   Second of September, we are at war, and all flown from the walls

1905   In gaslight (and was that gunfire?)  The copy is made

1843   "You will fancy some new film of the night has risen over
        The vastness of the departing form."

1838   The Fighting Temeraire, Tugged to her Last Berth to be Broken Up

1805   And what, pray, is England that expects?

*Note:*   *The dates which indicate narrative strands in the poem need not
        be spoken.
        The quotations are from John Ruskin's description of The Fighting
        Temeraire in Modern Painters*

# Letter from America

"                              - the rest you know"
Cooke's final words on Wednesday, closely placed
between the boom-mike and the showdown, spoken slow
for emphasis, nods closure to producer's glass screened face.

Nixon squats in Washington, hopes a change of heart
can coax congressional consent, that they can stitch
some votes of those who take the president's part
or else impeachment happens, events will turn the switch.

Thursday the president resigned - that we knew
by newsflash, while Letter from America on spool
had barely skimmed the tarmac, headed for the blue
for Friday, London, spun back ready to roll.

I heard Cooke that night, the voice recalled vibrates,
that old sly tone, lean, spare, insinuates.